The Pan

Written by Debbie Hepplewhite

Illustrated by Katie Rewse

RISING ★ STARS

Go to the tap, Pat.

Pat tips it into the pan.

Go to the tins, Pat.

Pat tips the tin into the pan.

Go to the pan, Nan!

Talk about the story

Ask your child these questions:

1 Who was Pat helping in the kitchen?

2 Where did Pat get the water from?

3 Who tipped the tin into the pan?

4 What do you think Nan did when she saw the pan boiling over?

5 What jobs do you help with at home?

6 Which is your favourite type of food to eat, and why do you like it?

Can your child retell the story in their own words?